Eight Yards, Down and Out

Other Fox Trot Books by Bill Amend

Fox Trot
Pass the Loot
Black Bart Says Draw

Anthology

Fox Trot: The Works

EIGHT YARDS, DOWN AND OUT

A Fox Trot Collection
by Bill Amend

Andrews and McMeel
A Universal Press Syndicate Company
Kansas City

Author's Note

The Sunday strips contained in this collection were originally created to run in color. To enhance their appearance for black and white reproduction, gray screens and solid black have been added where I felt it appropriate.

Most of the time, this poses no problems. However, two exceptions should be pointed out:

Page 34, panels 1 and 2—Jason's face should be a light blue.

Page 76, last panel—Jason's skin should, again, be a light blue.

So, to those of you with crayons. . .

5

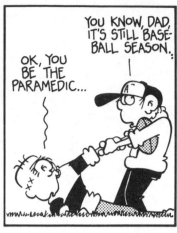

8

9

WHAT DO YOU HAVE FIRST PERIOD?

CURRENT AFFAIRS.

REALLY?! ME TOO!

ARE YOU SERIOUS?!

THIS IS GREAT! THIS IS PERFECT!

THANK YOU, O REGISTRAR GODS.

I'M PSYCHED. I WATCHED THE SHOW ALL SUMMER.

ME TOO. WHAT DO YOU HAVE AFTER IT?

AMEND

WELCOME TO CURRENT AFFAIRS, LADIES AND GENTLEMEN. MY NAME IS MS. PORTER AND I'LL BE YOUR TEACHER THIS SEMESTER. THAT SAID, LET'S BEGIN.

HOW MANY OF YOU HAVE BEEN FOLLOWING THE DRAMATIC EVENTS TAKING PLACE IN THE MIDDLE EAST THIS PAST MONTH?

AMEND

IRAQ? KUWAIT? SAUDI ARABIA? NO ONE KNOWS WHAT'S BEEN GOING **ON** THERE?!?

SPEAKING OF CRISES...

UM... I SAW "LAWRENCE OF ARABIA" ONCE. WELL, ACTUALLY, I TURNED IT OFF MIDWAY.

OK, NICOLE, I HAVE HERE A MAP OF THE WORLD WITH ALL OF THE COUNTRIES' NAMES REMOVED. WOULD YOU PLEASE POINT OUT TO THE CLASS WHERE IRAQ IS.

HMM...

WELL, LET'S SEE... IF THIS IS AMERICA...

THEN IRAQ MUST BE HERE.

AMEND

LET'S BACK UP TO THAT "IF," NICOLE.

OK, IF **THIS** IS AMERICA...

NICOLE, I FIND IT TRULY DISTRESSING THAT YOU CAN'T FIND EVEN YOUR OWN **COUNTRY** ON THIS MAP! — ALL THE NAMES ARE MISSING.

GO BY SHAPE.

HOW AM I SUPPOSED TO KNOW WHAT SORT OF STUPID SHAPE THE U.S. IS IN?!

INTERESTING CHOICE OF WORDS.

GIMME A HINT. IS THIS HAWAII OR AUSTRALIA?

OK, THIS **MUST** BE IRAQ. OR CUBA.

THAT'S ENOUGH GUESSING, NICOLE. PLEASE TAKE YOUR SEAT.

NOW, WILL SOMEONE PLEASE COME UP HERE AND **CORRECTLY** POINT OUT WHERE IRAQ IS ON THE MAP? PAIGE?

IT'S IN HERE SOMEWHERE.

BRAVO. DID EVERYONE SEE THAT?

CLAP CLAP CLAP

HOW THE HECK DID **YOU** KNOW?

IT WAS THE ONLY PLACE YOU HADN'T TRIED.

OK, THIS NEXT QUESTION IS FOR EVERYONE **EXCEPT** PAIGE...

WHATCHA READING?

THE NEWSPAPER.

I CAN SEE **THAT**.

MY CURRENT AFFAIRS TEACHER SAYS WE SHOULD SPEND AT LEAST 15 MINUTES A DAY READING IT.

THAT'S NOT A BAD IDEA.

SHE SAYS THAT IF WE DON'T KNOW WHAT'S GOING ON IN THE WORLD, WE'RE NOT REALLY LIVING IN IT. IT'S ACTUALLY KINDA FUN.

Cartoonist Solves Laura Palmer Murder "I'll be Danged", says Producer Lynch

SO WHAT'S GOING ON TODAY?

GARFIELD ATE JON'S LUNCH.

15

FoxTrot by Bill Amend

HUT TWO! HUT FOUR! HUT 16! HUT 256! HUT—...

LET'S SEE... 36... CARRY THE THREE...

MONTANA TAKES THE SNAP...

HE FAKES A HANDOFF TO CRAIG...

HE FAKES A LATERAL TO RATHMAN...

HE FAKES A PASS TO RICE...

HE FAKES A REVERSE TO TAYLOR...

THE DEFENSE, NO MATCH FOR THIS MASTER OF DECEPTION, STANDS UTTERLY MYSTIFIED...

NOT TO MENTION BORED SILLY!

HE FAKES A FUMBLE...

18

20

DENISE, **REALLY**, IT'S NO BIG DEAL.

I KNOW, BUT IT BUGS ME THAT YOU WOULD EVEN **CARE** ABOUT OTHER GIRLS.

IT'S A MATTER OF EGO FORTIFICATION. THE MORE GIRLS LIKE ME, THE BETTER I FEEL ABOUT MYSELF.

I LIKE YOU. ISN'T THAT ENOUGH?

AMEND

WELL, YEAH, BUT WHAT IF YOU'RE THE **ONLY** ONE WHO DOES? I NEED TO FIND THESE THINGS OUT.

PETER, I **KNOW** I'M NOT THE ONLY ONE WHO LIKES YOU.

REALLY? WHO ELSE DOES? ARE ANY OF THEM CHEERLEADERS?

PETER, LET'S TALK ABOUT **MY** EGO FOR A CHANGE...

LOOK, I DON'T WANT TO GET ALL STEAMED UP OVER THIS. IF YOU WANT TO LUST AFTER SOME GIRL IN YOUR GYM CLASS, BE MY GUEST. JUST REALIZE THAT IT HURTS MY FEELINGS.

AMEND

I'M NOT **LUSTING** AFTER HER. I JUST SAID SHE WAS BEAUTIFUL.

AMAZINGLY BEAUTIFUL.

REALLY AMAZINGLY BEAUTIFUL.

I **DIDN'T** WANT TO GET ALL STEAMED UP OVER THIS...

DENISE, I'M SORRY I HURT YOUR FEELINGS.

I DUNNO. SOMETIMES I GET ALL INSECURE ABOUT MYSELF. I GUESS THAT'S MY BIG PROBLEM.

I SHOULD JUST RECOGNIZE THAT YOU LIKE ME TONS AND BE HAPPY WITH THAT. I MEAN, HECK, THAT'S MORE THAN ENOUGH FOR **ANY** EGO.

YOU **DO** STILL LIKE ME TONS, DON'T YOU?

SOME MIGHT SAY THAT'S **MY** BIG PROBLEM.

AMEND

21

by Bill Amend

FoxTrot

WHAT WOULD **YOU** DO IF THIS WERE YOUR ASSIGNMENT?

BESIDES EAT IT...

WHATCHA DOING?

PONDERING.

ANYTHING IN PARTICULAR?

THIS CARDBOARD DIORAMA I'M SUPPOSED TO MAKE FOR SCHOOL.

OH? WHAT'S IT OF?

THAT'S THE PROBLEM. I'VE NARROWED IT DOWN TO EITHER CUSTER'S LAST STAND OR THE FRENCH REVOLUTION. I'M HAVING A HARD TIME CHOOSING.

AMEND

WHY DON'T YOU DO WHAT **I** DO WHEN I HAVE A TOUGH DECISION TO MAKE. WRITE UP A LIST OF THE PROS AND CONS.

I DID. IT'S STILL A TOUGH CALL.

WHAT HAVE YOU GOT DOWN?

CUSTER'S LAST STAND. PROS: LOTS OF ARROW-IMPALED BODIES. CONS: VERY FEW HEADLESS BODIES. THE FRENCH REVOLUTION. PROS: LOTS OF HEADLESS BODIES. CONS: VERY FEW ARROW-IMPALED BODIES.

LET ME ASK YOU THIS. DO WE HAVE A LOT OF TOOTHPICKS?

WHATCHA DOING?

PONDERING.

22

Row 1:

YOU LOOK EXCITED.

YOU **BET** I AM. MISS GRINCHLEY GAVE US AN EXTRA CREDIT HOMEWORK PROBLEM.

OH?

IT'S WORTH 10 QUIZ POINTS, ASSUMING ONE GETS IT RIGHT, WHICH I WILL.

WHY? IS IT EASY?

MOM, PLEASE. IT'S A MATH PROBLEM. THEY'RE **ALL** EASY FOR JASON FOX, HUMAN SUPERCOMPUTER.

AMEND

UNLIKE, SAY... MODESTY?

HEY, LET'S HAVE SOME FUN—READ ME THE QUESTION AND I'LL DO IT IN MY HEAD.

Row 2:

FIGURE IT OUT YET?

HMMMM...

JASON, YOU DON'T **HAVE** TO DO THIS PROBLEM IN YOUR HEAD.

OF **COURSE** I DO. OTHERWISE IT WOULDN'T BE A CHALLENGE.

AMEND

YOU'RE CHALLENGING MY **PATIENCE**. HERE—TAKE THE PROBLEM AND GO DO IT IN YOUR ROOM.

AAAA! DON'T **SHOW** IT TO ME! THAT CONSTITUTES A SECOND READING! I **NEVER** READ MATH QUESTIONS TWICE!

NEVER?!

WELL, MY MEMORY BEFORE AGE FIVE IS A LITTLE SHAKY, BUT...

Row 3:

JASON, I HAVE TO GET DINNER READY. TAKE THE PROBLEM AND DO IT IN YOUR ROOM.

BUT IF I DO IT IN MY ROOM, NO ONE'LL SEE ME **DO** IT!

NO ONE'LL KNOW HOW **EASY** IT WAS FOR ME! NO ONE'LL KNOW HOW **ASSUREDLY** I ARRIVED AT THE SOLUTION!

AMEND

NO ONE'LL KNOW HOW **QUICKLY** I DID IT!

BY THE SAME TOKEN...

TREK

23

STILL AT IT?

WHAT'S IT LOOK LIKE?!

JASON, IT'S JUST AN EXTRA CREDIT PROBLEM.

IT **WAS** JUST AN EXTRA CREDIT PROBLEM. NOW, UNFORTUNATELY, IT'S BECOMING SOMETHING MORE. SOMETHING SYMBOLIC. SOMETHING TERRIFYING.

WHAT'S THAT?

THE ONE MATH PROBLEM I COULDN'T DO.

...IN 10 MINUTES.

I MEAN, I'VE BEEN WORKING ON THIS THING FOR TWO **HOURS!**

JASON, I HATE TO SEE YOU THIS WORRIED OVER A SILLY MATH PROBLEM.

IT'S GONE BEYOND "WORRY," MOM.

IT'S GONE BEYOND "FEAR," IT'S GONE BEYOND "DISTRESS," IT'S GONE BEYOND "DISMAY."

IT'S GONE BEYOND "PANIC," IT'S GONE BEYOND "TERROR," IT'S GONE BEYOND "UTTER, TOTAL AND COMPLETE DESPERATION."

HAVE YOU ASKED YOUR FATHER FOR HELP?

IT HASN'T GONE THAT FAR.

POOR JASON.

WHAT'S WRONG?

HE'S BEEN TRYING TO DO THIS ONE MATH PROBLEM EVER SINCE HE GOT HOME AND HE JUST CAN'T GET THE ANSWER.

HMM. MUST BE SOME PROBLEM.

APPARENTLY. I WISH I COULD DO SOMETHING TO HELP HIM OUT. WHERE ARE YOU GOING?

TO LEND THE KID MY MATH EXPERTISE.

I GUESS I **CAN** DO SOMETHING.

WHAT ARE YOU DOING?! THESE ARE MY NEW PANTS!

I CAN'T BELIEVE I'M DOING THIS.

OK, NOW THESE LITTLE GUYS ARE YOUR PAWNS.

HOW DID I LET YOU TALK ME INTO THIS, DADDY?

IT WAS EITHER PLAY CHESS OR DO YOUR HOMEWORK, REMEMBER? NOW **THIS** BIG FELLA IS YOUR KING.

I SHOULD'VE PICKED HOMEWORK.

PAIGE, PLEASE— I'M TRYING TO TEACH YOU SOMETHING.

BELIEVE ME, I'M **LEARNING** SOMETHING.

NOW, PERSONALLY, I LIKE TO GIVE MY KING A PAT ON THE HEAD FOR GOOD LUCK.

AMEND

SO WHAT'S THE POINT OF THE GAME?

TO CHECK-MATE YOUR OPPONENT'S KING.

WHICH MEANS WHAT?

I LIKE TO SAY IT'S WHEN HE'S "UNDER ASSAULT WITH NO PLACE TO VAULT."

AMEND

PRETTY NIFTY DESCRIPTION, EH?

...OF MY SANITY.

YOUR MOTHER SAYS SHE CAN'T BELIEVE I ACTUALLY MADE THAT UP.

DADDY, LOOK, LET'S JUST GET THIS OVER WITH. WHO GOES FIRST?

WELL, THAT DEPENDS ON THE COLOR OF YOUR PIECES.

WOULD YOU LIKE TO HAVE THE PLAIN OL' WHITE ONES...

ORRR...WOULD YOU **INSTEAD** CHOOSE TO COMMAND THE FIERY RED, SCARLET BRI-GADE? PIECES OF BLAZING PROMINENCE! PIECES THAT INNATELY AND UNAMBIGUOUSLY OOZE POWER AND CONFI-DENCE! PIECES THAT SHOUT WITH EACH AND EVERY MOVE, "I AM A **WINNER!**"

AMEND

LET ME GUESS— WHITE GOES FIRST.

...AND YOUR SWEATER— RED WOULD GO **SO** WELL WITH IT...

by Bill Amend

FoxTrot

CLAP
CLAP CLAP
CLAP CLAP
CLAP CLAP

THANK YOU...
THANK YOU...

YOU KNOW WHAT I LIKE MOST ABOUT FALL?

CRUNCHING THROUGH LEAVES?

NOPE.

MAKING JACK-O'-LANTERNS?

NOPE.

GOING TO FOOTBALL GAMES?

BRRR—THIS WIND IS GETTING CHILLY.

HERE.

NOW WHERE WERE WE?...

AMEND

YOU FIGURED IT OUT.

GOING TO FOOTBALL GAMES? REALLY? ME TOO.

HEY, JASON—DO YOU STILL HAVE THAT HALLOWEEN MASK YOU WORE A COUPLE OF YEARS AGO?

YEAH, WHY?

I THOUGHT I'D WEAR IT TO STEVE'S PARTY.

BUT THAT'S A VIOLATION OF THE HALLOWEEN SPIRIT.

WHAT ARE YOU TALKING ABOUT?

YOU'RE SUPPOSED TO ALWAYS TRY TO DO SOMETHING NEW AND SCARY. IF YOU WEAR MY MASK, YOU'RE JUST IMITATING ME.

AMEND

AND THAT'S NOT NEW AND SCARY?

I MEAN, I UNDERSTAND THE ALLURE...

NOW, IT MAY BE TOO SMALL—I WORE IT WHEN I WAS 8.

OOO—I LIKE IT.

IT'S A HEMO-TRON. THEY WERE THE ALIENS IN THE MOVIE "CARNIVORTEX."

CAN'T SAY I EVER SAW IT.

OH, MAN, YOU'D REMEMBER IF YOU HAD. IT WAS GREAT. THIS BAND OF ASTRONAUTS LAND ON THIS PLANET AND GET THEIR HEADS RIPPED OFF.

NOW IF I CAN JUST GET THIS STUPID THING—...

AMEND

YEAH—KINDA LIKE THAT.

JASON, HOW DO I GET THIS OFF?!

IT'S STUCK?! PETER, I TOLD YOU IT'D BE TOO SMALL!

FINE, FINE. JUST GET ME SOME SCISSORS.

SCISSORS?! YOU DON'T THINK I'M GOING TO LET YOU CUT UP MY FAVORITE MASK, DO YOU?!

JASON, THIS THING IS LIKE A SUCTION CUP! I CAN'T GET IT OFF ANY OTHER WAY!

AMEND

LOOK, I'LL THINK OF SOMETHING. JUST DON'T HURT THE MASK.

WELL, YOU'D BETTER THINK FAST.

♪ KIDS—DINNER. ♪

HMMM.

DESPITE TEMPTATION TO THE CONTRARY.

OOO—LOOKS GOOD.

THANK YOU. SCARY, DON'T YOU THINK?

DEFINITELY.

I BASED IT ON A MONSTER. GUESS WHICH ONE.

JASON, I HAVE NO IDEA.

C'MON, IT'S **OBVIOUS**—THE REPTILIAN EYES...THE FLARING NOSTRILS...THE EVIL, SHARKLIKE MOUTH...

HMMM...

I'LL GIVE YOU A HINT. IMAGINE IT WITH A PONYTAIL.

AAAA! SO **THEN** WHAT DID YOU DO?...

OH, MOM—THE KIDS ARE GONNA **LOVE** YOU.

WHY'S THAT?

THIS **CANDY**. YOU'VE GOT **EVERYTHING**. HERSHEY'S KISSES... JUNIOR MINTS... PEANUT BUTTER CUPS...

YES, WELL, I SORT OF BROKE DOWN THIS YEAR.

IT'S ABOUT TIME. NORMALLY YOU JUST GIVE OUT THOSE ICKY LITTLE BOXES OF RAISINS.

I STILL PLAN TO.

HUH? SO WHO'S THE CANDY FOR?

AS I SAID, I HAD A LITTLE BREAKDOWN.

WELL, IT'S HALLOWEEN. THE SCARIEST NIGHT OF THE YEAR.

IT'S NOT **REALLY** SCARY.

HA! HOW LONG HAS IT BEEN SINCE **YOU'VE** BEEN OUT TRICK-OR-TREATING?

...WALKING STREET AFTER STREET... WITH WHO-KNOWS-WHO AROUND THE NEXT BEND... WITH A PRACTICALLY FULL MOON...

...WITH **DAD** AT YOUR SIDE?

OK, IT **IS** REALLY SCARY.

WE MEET AGAIN, OBI-WANOBI.

36

DID YOU SEE THIS?

WHAT?

THIS HEALTH CLUB IS HAVING A WINTER SPECIAL. SIX MONTHS FOR THE PRICE OF THREE.

SO?

SO THEY'VE GOT ROWING MACHINES, STAIRMASTERS, A WEIGHT ROOM— EVERYTHING A PERSON WOULD NEED TO GET IN SHAPE.

I DON'T THINK YOU'RE OUT OF SHAPE.

I'M NOT TALKING ABOUT ME.

IS PETER GETTING CHUNKY? I HADN'T NOTICED.

ROGER, I THINK YOU SHOULD LOOK INTO THIS HEALTH CLUB DEAL.

WHY?— YOU THINK I'M FAT?!

I'M NOT SAYING THAT, SILLY. I'M JUST SAYING THAT WORKING OUT SOME MIGHT BE GOOD FOR YOU.

HMMPH.

I MEAN, GOOD GRIEF, YOU DON'T HAVE TO BE FAT TO BENEFIT FROM EXERCISE!

WOULD YOU DO IT WITH ME?

WHY?— YOU THINK I'M FAT?!

GOOD GRIEF IS RIGHT...

ROGER, WHAT'S SO AWFUL ABOUT JOINING A HEALTH CLUB?

ARE YOU KIDDING? I'LL STICK OUT LIKE A SORE THUMB!

THAT'S NONSENSE.

IT'S TRUE! EVERYONE'LL BE STARING AT ME, WHISPERING AND POINTING WHILE I TRY TO WORK OUT. IT'S EMBARRASSING!

ROGER, YOU'RE NOT A FAT COW.

EXACTLY. I'LL BE BENCH-PRESSING SCHWARZENEGGERIAN BARBELLS WHILE EVERYONE ELSE IS PLODDING ALONG ON THEIR WIMPY TREADMILLS. I'LL LOOK LIKE A SHOW-OFF.

MAYBE YOU COULD, YOU KNOW, EASE INTO THOSE BIG WEIGHTS.

NOPE. A GUY LIKE ME CAN'T GO HALFWAY. MAYBE IN A FEW YEARS.

38

YOU REALLY THINK I'M OVERWEIGHT?

A LITTLE, YES. I MEAN, HECK, YOU'VE GAINED 10 POUNDS IN THE LAST TWO MONTHS.

THINK OF IT THIS WAY—THERE'S MORE OF ME TO LOVE!

MORE OF ME TO HUG! MORE OF ME TO TICKLE! MORE OF ME TO GRAB HOLD OF! MORE OF ME TO WORSHIP AND ADMIRE! MORE OF ME TO FILL YOUR DAYS AND NIGHTS WITH WARM AND DREAMY HAPPINESS!

AMEND

MORE OF YOU TO STARE AT IN UTTER DISBELIEF.

SO WHEN'S DINNER?

OK, ROGER, I'LL JOIN IF YOU'LL JOIN.

WHY ARE YOU SO EAGER FOR ME TO JOIN THIS STUPID HEALTH CLUB?

BECAUSE IT'D BE GOOD FOR YOUR HEART, IT'D BE GOOD FOR YOUR MIND, IT'D BE GOOD FOR YOUR SOUL...

IT'D MAKE YOU FEEL YOUNGER, IT'D MAKE YOU FEEL ENERGETIC, IT'D MAKE YOU FEEL **ALIVE**...

AND I'D GET HALF THE BED AGAIN.

WE **COULD** JUST GET A KING-SIZE...

AMEND

SO DID YOU AND DADDY JOIN THAT HEALTH CLUB?

OUCH. YES.

SORE MUSCLES?

MM-HMM. MY ARMS, MY BACK, MY LEGS...

WHAT ALL DID YOU DO??

BASICALLY, WE JUST WENT IN, SIGNED UP AND LEFT.

AMEND

DADDY STRUGGLED THAT MUCH, EH?

WORSE. HE WENT LIMP. YOU WOULDN'T KNOW WHERE THE HEATING PAD IS, WOULD YOU?

I'VE MADE AN APPOINTMENT FOR YOU TO SEE DR. WATSON TOMORROW.

DR. WATSON? WHY?

THE GUY AT THE HEALTH CLUB SAID YOU SHOULDN'T SUDDENLY START AN EXERCISE PROGRAM WITHOUT CONSULTING YOUR PHYSICIAN FIRST.

ANDY, I DON'T NEED SOME DOCTOR'S PERMISSION TO EXERCISE! LOOK AT ME!

UH HUH.

I MEAN, WHAT'S HE GONNA SAY?

AMEND

YOU DO, UH, HAVE A WILL, RIGHT?

YOU KNOW, THIS OFFICE DOESN'T SEEM AS CHILLY AS IT USED TO.

MR. FOX, NOT ONLY DO YOU NEED EXERCISE, I SUSPECT YOU NEED A MAJOR CHANGE IN DIET.

OH?

YOUR CHOLESTEROL LEVEL, BLOOD PRESSURE AND BODY FAT PERCENTAGE ARE ALL PRACTICALLY OFF THE SCALE. WHAT EXACTLY DO YOU EAT?

WELL, LET'S SEE. FOR BREAKFAST I'LL USUALLY HAVE A COUPLA THINGS OF COFFEE WHILE I READ THE PAPER...

AMEND

TWO CUPS OF COFFEE IS OK. WHAT ELSE?

POTS, NOT CUPS.

LYNN, COULD YOU TELL MRS. O'GRADY SHE MAY WANT TO RESCHEDULE?

THEN I'LL CRACK OPEN A PACK OF BACON...

OK, NOW I WANT YOU TO KEEP YOUR WORKOUTS MODERATE AT FIRST. NOTHING OVER 30 MINUTES.

THIRTY MINUTES. GOT IT.

AND REMEMBER TO MONITOR YOUR PULSE. TRY TO KEEP IT IN THE RANGE WE DISCUSSED.

MONITOR PULSE. GOT IT.

THE BOOKLET I GAVE YOU SHOULD ADDRESS MOST OF YOUR OTHER QUESTIONS.

IT DOESN'T SAY ANYTHING ABOUT WEIGHT LIFTING.

IN YOUR CASE, CHECK UNDER "WALKING."

NO NO—I MEAN, LIKE, DUMBBELLS.

SO WHAT'D THE DOCTOR SAY?

HE SAID EVERYTHING I **DIDN'T** WANT TO HEAR.

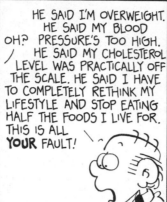

OH? HE SAID I'M OVERWEIGHT. HE SAID MY BLOOD PRESSURE'S TOO HIGH. HE SAID MY CHOLESTEROL LEVEL WAS PRACTICALLY OFF THE SCALE. HE SAID I HAVE TO COMPLETELY RETHINK MY LIFESTYLE AND STOP EATING HALF THE FOODS I LIVE FOR. THIS IS ALL **YOUR** FAULT!

MY FAULT?!

YOU'RE THE ONE WHO MADE ME GO **SEE** HIM!

GOSH, WHAT **WAS** I THINKING?

DID IT EVER OCCUR TO YOU THAT MAYBE I **LIKED** MY LIFE?!

AMEND

OK, SET THE RESISTANCE LEVEL TO "MODERATE".

NO SWEAT.

TIME LIMIT 30 MI.

NOW SET THE TIMER FOR 20 MINUTES.

NO SWEAT.

TIME LIMIT 30 MI.

NOW PEDAL.

PEDAL?

AS IN SWEAT.

YOU KNOW, I THINK I COULD USE A LITTLE MORE STRETCHING...

TIME LIMIT 30 MI.

UGGH. I FEEL LIKE DEATH INCARNATE.

ROGER, WHAT DID YOU EXPECT?

I DIDN'T EXPECT **THIS**. MY THROAT'S ALL DRY... I FEEL NAUSEATED... WEAK... I THINK I'VE GONE THROUGH 12 GLASSES OF WATER...

IT'S YOUR FIRST TIME. IT'LL GET EASIER.

IT'D **BETTER**.

I MEAN, WHEN **WAS** THE LAST TIME YOU DID ANY EXERCISE?

EXERCISE? I'M TALKING ABOUT EATING THESE STUPID RICE CAKES.

OH. WELL, HERE — SPRINKLE SOME WHEAT GERM ON IT.

AMEND

42

FourTrot

by Bill Amend

FOURTH AND GOAL. TWO SECONDS LEFT ON THE CLOCK. CAN PETER FOX PULL OFF A MIRACLE?

FOR THE ANSWER, LET'S CHECK IN WITH OUR HEAD STATISTICIAN...

PETER FOX TAKES THE SNAP...

HE LOOKS LEFT... HE LOOKS RIGHT...

HE PASSES TO HIM-SELF... THE DEFENSE IS STUNNED...

HE SPOTS HIS CHANCE... HE LEAPS OVER THE CHARGING LINEBACKERS...

TOUCHDOWN! THE CHEERLEADERS SWARM THEIR HERO...

TO THINK I SHARE HIS GENES.

TO THINK I SHARE **BOTH** YOUR GENES.

TO THINK I HELPED **GIVE** HIM THOSE GENES.

YO, PETE! I'M OPEN!

AMEND

44

MOM, CAN I BORROW SOME PAPER?

SURE. WHAT FOR?

I'M WRITING UP MY LIST OF THINGS I WANT FOR CHRISTMAS.

JASON, IT WAS JUST THANKS-GIVING! ISN'T IT A LITTLE SOON TO BE THINKING ABOUT THAT?

AMEND

ARE YOU KIDDING? THERE'S HARDLY ENOUGH TIME LEFT AS IT IS.

WHAT? FOR PEOPLE TO SHOP?

FOR ME TO WRITE IT ALL DOWN.

GOSH, YOU KNOW, I'VE ONLY GOT TWO REAMS LEFT...

HEY, PETER—HOW DO YOU SPELL "BALLISTIC"?

B-A-L-L-I-S-T-I-C.

AMEND

HOW DO YOU SPELL "NEUTRON"?

N-E-U-T-R-O-N.

IS "WARHEAD" HYPHENATED?

NO.

WHAT'S SANTA'S ZIP CODE?

YOU KNOW, YOU MAY NOT WANT TO BE HERE FOR CHRISTMAS.

HEY, JASON—HOW DO YOU SPELL "GIVE IT UP, YOU LITTLE NERD BAG"?!

HEY, DAD—IS "FERRARI" SPELLED F-E-R-R-A-R-I?

I'M PRETTY SURE. WHY?

I'M WRITING UP MY CHRISTMAS LIST.

AREN'T YOU A LITTLE **YOUNG** TO BE ASKING FOR A FERRARI?

AMEND

I FIGURED IF I GOT ONE, YOU COULD USE IT UNTIL I TURN 16.

BUT HE'S BEEN SO **GOOD** THIS YEAR.

HAVE YOU LOST YOUR **MIND**?!

47

HEY, PAIGE— WHAT DO YOU WANT FOR CHRISTMAS?

I DUNNO. NEW SUNGLASSES... A WATCH... A LEATHER JACKET... WHY?

I'M TRYING TO FIGURE OUT WHAT TO ASK SANTA FOR FOR CHRISTMAS.

SO WHY'D YOU ASK WHAT **I** WANT?

I WANT TO GET THE ANTI-MATTER VERSIONS OF YOUR PRESENTS. THAT WAY, WHEN THEY COME INTO CONTACT WITH **YOUR** STUFF, IT'LL ALL BLOW UP. HAVEN'T YOU EVER SEEN "STAR TREK"?

AMEND

NOW, THEN, WAS THERE A PARTICULAR **STYLE** OF SUNGLASSES YOU WANTED?

TELL ME, DO **YOU** COME IN AN ANTI-MATTER VERSION?

MOM, CAN I USE YOUR COMPUTER FOR A WHILE?

WHY?

WELL, TO HELP SANTA OUT, I'VE MADE A GRAPH OF MY "GOODNESS" OVER THE PAST 11 MONTHS AND I THINK IT'D BE MORE EFFECTIVE IF I RENDERED IT WITH THE COMPUTER. SOMEHOW, CRAYON DOESN'T QUITE CUT IT.

CAN I SEE?

ESSENTIALLY, I DEPICT MY YEAR AS A FLUCTUATION BETWEEN "VERY, VERY GOOD" AND "AMAZINGLY GOOD" WITH A COUPLA SPIKES TOUCHING ON "NONE BETTER."

YOU KNOW THE SAYING "COMPUTERS DON'T LIE"? I MEAN, THAT'S JUST A **SAYING**, RIGHT?

YOU DON'T MIND IF I ADD **TODAY'S** DATA POINT, DO YOU?

AMEND

SO HOW'S THE BIG CHRISTMAS LIST COMING?

GOOD. I WISH I COULD BE THERE TO SEE SANTA'S FACE WHEN HE GETS IT.

WHY'S THAT?

DAD, IT'S PRACTICALLY A WORK OF ART. I'VE GOT IT ALPHABETIZED, ILLUSTRATED, PRIORITY-CODED AND INDEXED BY CATEGORY. THE INDEX ALONE TOOK ME TWO DAYS.

SO WHERE IS IT?

OVER THERE IN THE CORNER.

AMEND

NO WONDER YOU NEED AN INDEX.

DAD, THAT **IS** THE INDEX. SAY, YOU WOULDN'T KNOW ANYTHING ABOUT FREIGHT CARRIERS, WOULD YOU?

by Bill Amend

FoxTrot

YOU GOTTA FEEL SORRY FOR THE WEATHERMAN.

WHY'S THAT?

HE SAID IT WOULDN'T SNOW THIS WEEK.

WELL, IF WE DON'T HURRY UP WITH THIS, IT **WON'T**.

WHAT **ARE** YOU **DOING**?!

IT'S OUR VERSION OF THE ANCIENT EGYPTIAN SNOW DANCE.

HUMMINA... HUMMINA...

WHAT ANCIENT EGYPTIAN SNOW DANCE?!

MARCUS MADE IT UP. WE'VE DECIDED THAT IN OUR PAST LIVES I WAS LEONARDO DA VINCI AND MARCUS WAS KING CHEOPS.

HUMMINA...

YOU ARE SO **WEIRD**!

LAUGH ALL YOU WANT, BUT WHEN WE DID IT **LAST** YEAR IT SNOWED TWO DAYS LATER.

HUMMINA... HUMMINA...

AND THAT COULDN'T HAVE BEEN JUST MERE **COINCIDENCE**?!

MAYBE. BUT WE THINK IT'S WORTH THE EFFORT.

HUMMINA...

IT'S WORTH MAKING COMPLETE **IDIOTS** OF YOURSELVES FOR THE **CHANCE** THAT IT MIGHT SNOW AS A RESULT?!

THEY ALSO CLOSED SCHOOL TWO DAYS LATER.

HUMMINA...

HUMMINA... HUMMINA...

HUMMINA... HUMMINA...

AMEND

HUMMINA...

NOW KICK WITH YOUR RIGHT FOOT EVERY SEVENTH "HUMMINA."

TELL HER ABOUT THE HEAD THRUSTS— WE DON'T WANT LOCUSTS.

UNBELIEVABLE. SIMPLY UNBELIEVABLE.

WHAT?

DID PETER TELL YOU WHAT HE DID?! I'LL TELL YOU— HE PUT A STUPID AD IN THE STUPID SCHOOL PAPER TELLING PEOPLE TO ASK ME TO THE STUPID DANCE!

WHY WOULD HE DO THAT?

BECAUSE HE'S A STUPID SCUM CHEWER. I CAN'T IMAGINE FEELING MORE HUMILIATED THAN I DO RIGHT NOW.

AMEND

SO, I'VE PROBABLY GOT A MILE-HIGH STACK OF MESSAGES, HUH?

UH...

STILL MAD AT PETER?

NO. I'M JUST FRUSTRATED.

ABOUT THE DANCE?

YES! I MEAN, EVEN WITH THAT STUPID AD, NOBODY'S ASKED ME TO GO WITH THEM! WHAT'S WRONG WITH ME?! WHAT'S WRONG WITH THEM?!

AMEND

PAIGE, MAYBE YOU SHOULD STOP ALL THIS SPECULATING AND SIMPLY ASK SOMEONE YOURSELF.

HMMM...

WHAT??

I SAID, WHAT'S WRONG WITH YOU?!

HOW WAS SCHOOL?

FINE.

ANY, UH, PROGRESS ON THE DANCE FRONT?

YOU COULD SAY THAT. NICOLE AND I DECIDED TO FOLLOW YOUR ADVICE, SO AT LUNCH WE ASKED THE FENUCCHI TWINS IF THEY'D GO WITH US.

WHAT'D THEY SAY?

"GOLLY, GOSH DANG, GEE WHIZ, YES!"

THAT'S GREAT!

NEEDLESS TO SAY, WE RESCINDED OUR OFFER. BUT CONFIDENCE IS HIGH...

AMEND

54

WHERE ARE YOU OFF TO?

JASON AND I THOUGHT WE'D ...UH...

...ER... UM... UH...

AMEND

PAIGE ISN'T HOME.

...GO SHOPPING.

DID YOU JUST HEAR SOMETHING?

IS IT REAL BUTTER OR FAKE BUTTER?

SO WHAT SHOULD WE GET DAD?

HE LIKES FOOTBALL— GET HIM ONE OF THESE JERRY RICE NIGHT-LIGHTS.

CLARK
22

20% OFF

YOU'RE KIDDING, RIGHT?

NO. WHY?

20% OFF

JASON, WE CAN'T GIVE DAD A STUPID JERRY RICE NIGHT-LIGHT FOR CHRISTMAS!

I GUESS IT IS PRETTY LAME, HUH?

AMEND

REGARDLESS. WE GAVE HIM ONE FOR HIS BIRTHDAY.

DOES HE LIKE HOCKEY? HERE'S A WAYNE GRETSKY VERSION.

20% OFF

WANNA SPLIT UP FOR A WHILE? I NEED TO GET SOMETHING FOR YOU.

FINE. MEET HERE IN 20 MINUTES?

OK. AND DON'T TRY FOLLOWING ME.

PETER, GET REAL—THAT'S SO FAR BENEATH ME.

MALL DIRECTORY

LOWER LEVEL

ZOOM IN ON CAMERA FOUR.

KID, C'MON— YOU'RE NOT EVEN SUPPOSED TO BE IN HERE.

SECU

AMEND

60

by Bill Amend

FoxTrot

LUKE, **I** AM YOUR FATHER!

NOW, SON, ABOUT THIS SPEEDING THROUGH THE GALAXY BUSINESS...

LUKE SKYWALKER AND OBI-WAN KENOBI EXPLORE THE PLANET'S SURFACE IN THEIR TRUSTY LANDSPEEDER.

SUDDENLY, A GIANT IGUANO-BEAST BLOCKS THEIR WAY! WHAT **WILL** THEY DO?!

LUKE TRIES THE FORCE.

IT'S NO USE. HE RUNS.

OBI-WAN TRIES THE FORCE.

IT'S NO USE. HE RUNS.

THE IGUANO-BEAST TRIES THE LANDSPEEDER.

YOU'D **BETTER** RUN...

AMEND.

SO HAVE YOU MADE A NEW YEAR'S RESOLUTION?

YUP. 1991'S GONNA BE THE YEAR I MAKE MY FIRST MILLION.

JASON, C'MON — YOU'RE SUPPOSED TO MAKE RESOLUTIONS THAT ARE AT LEAST **SLIGHTLY** REALISTIC.

SUCH AS?

I DUNNO. I THOUGHT MAYBE YOU COULD TRY BEING A LITTLE NICER TO YOUR SISTER.

AND YOU THINK **THAT'S** REALISTIC?!

HUMOR ME.

YOU KNOW... IF YOU WERE TO, SAY, **PAY** ME...

LOOK, KIDS, I'M NOT ASKING YOU TO BE BEST FRIENDS OR ANYTHING; I'M SIMPLY SUGGESTING THAT YOU TRY BEING **NICE** TO EACH OTHER FOR A CHANGE.

IT'S IMPOSSIBLE!

WELL, SURE, IF YOU THINK OF IT AS SOMETHING ENDLESS. THE TRICK IS TO BREAK IT DOWN INTO MANAGEABLE INCREMENTS.

YOU KNOW, TAKE IT ONE DAY AT A TIME.

A WHOLE DAY?!

ONE **HOUR** AT A TIME?

A WHOLE HOUR?!

AND HOW WAS **YOUR** DAY?

NNGH.

WHAT'S THE MATTER?

OH, IT'S JASON AND PAIGE. FOR THEIR NEW YEAR'S RESOLUTIONS THEY PROMISED TO TRY TO BE NICE TO EACH OTHER.

AND IT'S NOT WORKING?

NOT IN THE WAY I'D HOPED.

EXCUSE ME, SIS, BUT MY FRIEND QUINCY HERE WANTED A CLOSER LOOK AT YOUR LOVELY VISAGE.

NO PROBLEM, LITTLE BUDDY. LET ME JUST AIM MY FOOT TOWARD YOUR HANDSOME TEETH.

63

DENISE, I CAN'T **DO** THIS!

WHY? YOU'RE DOING FINE.

YOUR PARENTS ARE PAYING ME TO HELP YOU **STUDY**, NOT TO SIT HERE AND **KISS** YOU!

BUT YOU **ARE** HELPING ME STUDY. BY KISSING ME AFTER A CORRECT ANSWER, YOU'RE INSTILLING IN ME A DESIRE TO DO WELL, A DESIRE TO LEARN.

AMEND

I SUPPOSE.

NOW STOP BEING A GEEK AND READ ME SOME MORE QUESTIONS.

LET'S SEE... THE FRENCH REVOLUTION...

CAN WE DO THE RENAISSANCE AGAIN? I DIDN'T MISS ONE OF THOSE.

DENISE, I FEEL LIKE A GIGOLO.

A GIGOLO?!

WELL, YEAH. ESSENTIALLY I'M GETTING PAID TO SIT HERE AND KISS YOU. I'M **SUPPOSED** TO BE TUTORING YOU.

I CAN THINK OF WORSE WAYS TO EARN A FEW BUCKS.

AMEND

TRUE.

LOOK, IF THIS REALLY MAKES YOU UNCOMFORTABLE, WE'LL JUST DO IT NORMALLY.

NO KISSING?

NO, NO– NO MONEY.

WHERE HAVE **YOU** BEEN ALL AFTERNOON?

I WAS OVER TUTORING DENISE.

AH, YES— I SHOULD HAVE SURMISED THAT. THE FRAZZLED DEMEANOR...

BIG-TIME FRAZZLED.

THE WEARY-LOOKING EYES...

BIG-TIME WEARY.

THE LIPSTICK-STAINED CHEEKS...

SO, UH, WHEN'S DINNER?

AMEND

66

SO HOW'S SUPER MARIO GOING?

HORRIBLY. I JUST DIED ON WORLD SEVEN. I DON'T KNOW HOW MARCUS DID IT.

JASON, YOU KNOW, MAYBE THE REASON MARCUS WAS ABLE TO FINISH SUPER MARIO IS THAT HE SPENT ALL HIS TIME **PLAYING** IT.

WHILE YOU WERE LEADING A HEALTHY, SEMI-**NORMAL** LIFE, HE WAS PROBABLY NEGLECTING HIS HOMEWORK, MISSING OUT ON SLEEP, SKIPPING MEALS...

AMEND

HE PROBABLY STOPPED SOCIALIZING ALTOGETHER...

MOM, CAN I GO GET SOME PAPER? I WANT TO WRITE THESE THINGS DOWN.

DING DING BLOOP

DING DING

DING DING BEEP BEEP BEEP

YOU'RE UP AWFULLY EARLY.

TECHNICALLY, I'M UP AWFULLY LATE.

DING DING

AMEND

YOU WERE UP ALL **NIGHT**?!

I DIDN'T **PLAN** TO BE.

JASON, THIS NINTENDO THING HAS GOTTEN **WAY** OUT OF HAND!

MOM, C'MON— IF I'M GONNA CATCH UP TO MARCUS, I'VE **GOT** TO PUT IN SOME SERIOUS HOURS.

YOU'RE NOT **GOING** TO CATCH UP TO MARCUS.

OH, FINE. **BE** A PESSIMIST.

AMEND

TRY "REALIST."

HEY— WHY ARE YOU UNPLUGGING THE MACHINE?!

FoxTrot

Give Jason all your money

SO WHAT DO YOU THINK OF MY FLIP-BOOK? SAY... ISN'T THIS YOUR NEW **PURSE**?...

PROMISE ME YOU WON'T SHOW THIS THING TO YOUR FATHER.

SON, I'VE BEEN THINKING...

FLIP FLIP FLIP

AMEND

MOM, YOU CAN'T **DO** THIS!

I MOST CERTAINLY **CAN**.

IF YOU TAKE AWAY MY NINTENDO, I'LL **DIE!**

YOU SHOULD HAVE THOUGHT OF THAT **BEFORE** YOU PULLED THIS LITTLE STUNT.

AMEND

I'LL WITHER AWAY! I'LL LOSE DIRECTION IN MY LIFE! I'LL BE ALONE IN A BLEAK, COLD AND HOSTILE WORLD!

SO WEAR A SWEATER.

LOOK AT MY THUMBS! THEY'RE... THEY'RE... THEY'RE **TWITCHING!** MOM, **PLEASE!**

DAD, YOU'VE GOTTA GO TALK SOME SENSE INTO MOM.

WHY?

WHY?! SHE TOOK AWAY MY NINTENDO! I MEAN, SO I STAYED UP ALL NIGHT PLAYING IT—BIG DEAL!

HOW LONG DID SHE TAKE IT AWAY FOR?

TWO LOUSY WEEKS.

TWO WEEKS?! ANDY...

PULL NO PUNCHES, DAD!

I THOUGHT WE AGREED IT'D BE **MONTHS!**...

AMEND

I HATE MOM.

WHAT'D SHE DO NOW?

WHAT'D SHE DO?! YOU WANNA KNOW WHAT SHE DID?!—THINK UNSPEAKABLE. AND THINK NINTENDO.

No!

YES.

SHE **DIDN'T!**

AMEND

SHE **DID**. SHE TOOK IT AWAY.

OH. I THOUGHT SHE BOUGHT YOU MORE CARTRIDGES.

YOU'RE GOING SLEDDING **WHERE**?

KAMIKAZE RIDGE. SOME KIDS AT SCHOOL DISCOVERED IT. IT'S OVER BY THE RESERVOIR.

THAT'S PRETTY FAR AWAY. HOW ARE YOU GETTING THERE?

PETER. HE SAID HE'D DRIVE ME TO **CHINA** IF IT MEANT SEEING ME DIE IN A CLOUD OF SNOW.

I **GUESS** I SHOULD BE FLATTERED.

I **KNOW** I SHOULD BE **WORRIED**.

SAY, DOES DAD STILL HAVE THAT FOOTBALL HELMET?

WELL, THERE SHE IS. KAMIKAZE RIDGE.

YUP.

THERE SHE IS. THE PATH BACK TO THE CAR.

YUP.

WHAT DO YOU MEAN, "**WE'D** BETTER GET STARTED"?!

WELL, I'M NOT DOING THIS **ALONE**.

JASON, THE ONLY REASON I CAME OUT HERE WITH YOU WAS TO **WATCH** YOU DIE — I NEVER SAID ANYTHING ABOUT GETTING ON THE SLED **WITH** YOU!

THINK OF THE GLORY!

THINK CHUCK YEAGER! THINK ALAN SHEPARD! THINK EVEL KNIEVEL!

THINK OPENING CREDITS OF "WIDE WORLD OF SPORTS."

BABES, PETER. THINK OF WHAT THE **BABES** WILL SAY...

BRRR!

MMM.

I SAID BRRR.

I SAID MMM.

MAN, IS IT **COLD** OUTSIDE!

MMM.

AND I DON'T MEAN REGULAR COLD—I MEAN BONE-CHILLING, ICY COLD.

MMM.

I'D ESTIMATE THAT WITH THE WIND CHILL FACTORED IN, IT'S ABOUT THREE DEGREES OUT THERE.

MMM.

...KELVIN.

MMM.

I MEAN, I WAS OUTSIDE FOR ALL OF 20 MINUTES AND I CONSIDER MYSELF LUCKY TO BE ALIVE.

MMM.

ESPECIALLY SINCE I WAS ONLY WEARING A T-SHIRT.

MMM.

MOM, C'MON—YOU'RE SUPPOSED TO TURN AROUND!

JASON, I **SAW** YOU GETTING YOUR HALLOWEEN MAKEUP OUT OF THE ATTIC...

AMEND

ROGER, ARE THE CHICAGO BULLS A GOOD TEAM TO WATCH PLAY?

ABSOLUTELY.

LIVE?

ABSOLUTELY.

SO IF SOMEONE WERE TO, SAY, OFFER YOU A TICKET TO GO SEE THEM, YOU'D GO?

YES! YES! YES! YES! SOMEONE'S OFFERING ME A TICKET?!

LET ME BE MORE SPECIFIC WITH MY PRONOUNS...

HEE HEE — FRED'S GONNA DIE WHEN I TELL HIM.

AMEND

WHAT DO YOU MEAN IT'S NOT FAIR?! MY EDITOR INVITED ME!

ANDY, I LIVE FOR BASKETBALL! IF ANYONE DESERVES THIS TICKET, I DO!

ROGER, I'VE NEVER BEEN TO A BASKETBALL GAME BEFORE.

EXACTLY. YOU WON'T BE ABLE TO APPRECIATE IT! THIS IS GOING TO BE ONE OF THE BEST HOME GAMES OF THE YEAR AND YOU WON'T HAVE EVEN THE SLIGHTEST CLUE AS TO WHAT'S GOING ON!

AMEND

YOU DON'T KNOW THE TEAMS... YOU DON'T KNOW THE PLAYERS... YOU DON'T KNOW THE STRATEGIES... YOU DON'T KNOW THE GAME!

I KNOW HOW TO DO "THE WAVE."...

ANDY, THERE'S A BUTCHER KNIFE ON THE COUNTER. IT'D BE QUICKER.

YO, DAD — WHAT'S WRONG?

YOUR MOTHER'S GOING TO THE BASKETBALL GAME FRIDAY NIGHT.

THE BULLS GAME?! WITHOUT YOU?!

UH HUH. HER EDITOR HAD ONLY ONE EXTRA TICKET.

I DON'T THINK MOM EVEN KNOWS WHAT A BASKETBALL LOOKS LIKE! AND YOU HAVE TO STAY HOME?! THIS MUST HURT. THIS MUST REALLY, REALLY HURT.

TELL ME ABOUT IT.

WELL, FOR STARTERS, YOUR STOMACH'S PROBABLY—...

LET'S CONCENTRATE ON MY EARS FOR THE TIME BEING.

AMEND

DADDY, I AM APPALLED!

WHAT ABOUT?

PETER JUST TOLD ME YOU'RE MAD BECAUSE MOM'S GOING TO A DUMB OL' BASKETBALL GAME WITHOUT YOU. YOU SHOULD BE ASHAMED OF YOURSELF!

PAIGE, IT'S NOT A "DUMB OL'" BASKETBALL GAME, IT'S THE **BULLS** GAME!

SO YOU SHOULD BE **HAPPY** THAT MOM GETS TO GO!

I'D BE HAPPY IF SHE HAD ANY SORT OF KNOWLEDGE OF BASKETBALL! AS IT IS, THE TICKET'S PRACTICALLY GOING TO BE WASTED ON HER.

IF IT MAKES HER HAPPY, IT'S NOT A WASTE.

I, ON THE OTHER HAND, CAN APPRECIATE—...

YOU KNOW WHAT **I** WOULD APPRECIATE?...

MAN, DAD, YOU WERE PRETTY MELLOW WHEN MOM LEFT FOR THE GAME.

WELL, SHE AND I TALKED ABOUT IT LAST NIGHT.

I REALIZED WHAT A JERK I WAS BEING. I MEAN, WHY **SHOULDN'T** SHE GO? IT'S HER **TICKET**.

SO WHAT IF SHE DOESN'T KNOW BASKETBALL. SO WHAT IF SHE DOESN'T KNOW WHO'S WHO. SO WHAT IF SHE CAN'T TELL A LOW POST FROM A HIGH POST.

SO WHAT IF MICHAEL JORDAN DIVES INTO HER LAP.

THAT WOULD'VE BEEN MY **SEAT**! AAAA!

(YAWN) BOY, AM I **POOPED**!

SO HOW'D YOU LIKE THE GAME?

IT WAS FUN. THIS BIG, BALD CHICAGO PLAYER FELL INTO MY LAP AND AFTERWARD I TALKED HIM INTO GIVING ME AN AUTOGRAPHED BALL.

YOU GOT A BASKETBALL SIGNED BY MICHAEL JORDAN?!

I THOUGHT IT WAS THE LEAST HE COULD DO— HE GOT SWEAT ALL OVER MY SKIRT.

I CAN'T BELIEVE THIS! FIRST YOU'RE GIVEN A FRONT-ROW TICKET TO THE BEST GAME EVER, **THEN** MICHAEL JORDAN DIVES INTO YOUR LAP ON TV! **THEN** YOU TELL ME HE AUTOGRAPHS A BALL FOR YOU! **HOW** CAN YOU BE SO **LUCKY**?!

YOU MIGHT ASK HOW DID **YOU** GET SO LUCKY.

IT SAYS "TO ROGER"...

MAN...

WHAT'S WITH YOU?

TODAY MISS GRINCHLY SAID WE HAVE TO GIVE EVERYONE IN THE CLASS VALENTINE'S DAY CARDS. DO YOU KNOW HOW LONG IT'S GONNA TAKE TO CUSTOM-MAKE 30 CARDS?!

JUST GO TO THE STORE AND BUY 'EM. THAT'S WHAT I ALWAYS DO.

AMEND

AND DO THE GIRLS LIKE THEM?

ABSOLUTELY.

PASS THE CRAYONS.

MAN...

WHERE'S JASON? I HAVEN'T SEEN HIM ALL EVENING.

HE'S UP IN HIS ROOM MAKING VALENTINE'S DAY CARDS FOR THE KIDS IN HIS CLASS.

THAT SOUNDS LIKE A LOT OF WORK. WHY DOESN'T HE JUST BUY SOME?

HE SAYS STORE-BOUGHT CARDS ARE TOO, UH-WHAT'S THE WORD HE USED?...

MUSHY?   NO...

SENTIMENTAL?   NO...

CUTESY?   NO...

AMEND

IS "LARD-BUTT" HYPHEN-ATED?

CIVIL?   BINGO.

HOW ARE THE CARDS COMING ALONG?

SLOWLY. I DON'T KNOW HOW HALLMARK DOES IT.

JASON, THIS IS DIS-GUSTING!

THAT'S ONE OF MY PERSONAL FAVORITES. I BASED THE DRAWING ON THAT SCENE IN "INDIANA JONES AND THE TEMPLE OF DOOM" WHERE THE HIGH PRIEST STICKS HIS HAND INTO THE GUY'S CHEST CAVITY.

AMEND

"YOU STOLE MY HEART, VALENTINE."

NOTE THE HIGH-GLOSS PAINT FOR THE BLOOD.

I KNOW HOW HALLMARK DOESN'T DO IT.

OUT OF CURIOSITY, HOW MANY RIBS DO PEOPLE HAVE?

FoxTrot by Bill Amend

BASEBALL? PETER **KNOWS** BASEBALL.

DREAM ON.

I **WILL**, THANK YOU.

PETER **KNOWS** FOOTBALL.

PETER KNOWS BASKETBALL.

PETER KNOWS TENNIS.

PETER KNOWS NUNCHUCKS.

PETER KNOWS MOUNTAINEERING.

AMEND

PETER KNOWS FLYING.

BUT DOES PETER KNOW **PHYSICS?**

ZZZZ... PETER KNOWS CINDY CRAWFORD... ZZZZ...

AREN'T YOU A LITTLE **OLD** FOR PLAY-DOH?

I'M DOING THIS FOR SCHOOL.

WHAT? MAKING LITTLE MONSTERS?!

THEY'RE DINOSAURS. WE'RE SUPPOSED TO DO A REPORT ON THEIR DEMISE. I'M DOING MINE IN STOP-MOTION ANIMATION.

YOU'RE SO WEIRD. SO WHAT **DID** KILL THE DINOSAURS, ANYWAY?

WELL, SINCE NOBODY KNOWS FOR SURE, I'VE DECIDED TO PRESENT A **NEW** THEORY...

G.I. JOE?!

HEY— **YOU** TRY ANIMATING GLOBAL COOLING.

AMEND

MOM, AS YOU MAY HAVE HEARD, I'M MAKING AN ANIMATED FILM PRESENTATION FOR SCHOOL.

PAIGE TOLD ME. YES.

WELL, IT OCCURS TO ME THAT AS A PROFESSIONAL WRITER YOU MIGHT BE ABLE TO OFFER ME SOME ASSISTANCE.

I SEE.

I MEAN, LET'S BE HONEST— THERE ARE SOME THINGS THAT YOU CAN DO WITH A PEN, WORDS THAT YOU CAN PUT DOWN, THAT I PLAINLY AND SIMPLY CANNOT.

IS THAT WHY YOU'RE HOLDING MY CHECKBOOK?

AMEND

I'LL PUT YOU IN THE CREDITS...

IT'S THE DEBITS THAT CONCERN ME.

HEY, PETER— WANNA HELP ME WITH MY MOVIE?

I CAN'T. I'VE GOT A PAPER TO WRITE.

C'MON— I NEED YOU TO WORK THE CAMERA WHILE I ANIMATE THE DINO- SAURS.

HOW LONG WILL IT TAKE?

A HALF-HOUR. **TOPS.**

AMEND

...PER FRAME.

I CAN'T REMEM- BER— WAS THE BRACHIOSAURUS BREATHING **OUT** OR BREATHING **IN?**

AAAAAAAA!

WHAT'D I DO?! WHAT'D I DO?!

NOTHING. IT'S THIS STUPID **BOOK**!

RATS.

MR. THORNTON IS **SUCH A DINK**!

WHY'S THAT?

HE EXPECTS US TO READ "A TALE OF TWO CITIES" IN ONE WEEK! A 500-PAGE BOOK IN A **WEEK**!

I READ IT IN ONE WEEK.

YEAH, BUT I'LL BET YOU DIDN'T **ALSO** HAVE TO WRITE A STUPID **ESSAY** ON IT!

I DID TOO.

FIVE PAGES?!

FIVE PAGES.

SINGLE SPACED?!

SINGLE SPACED.

ABOUT SOME STUPID LADY WHO KNITS ALL THE TIME?!

MADAME DEFARGE. YUP.

AMEND

MY BROTHER IS **SUCH A DINK**!

PAIGE, EVEN IF I **HADN'T** THROWN IT AWAY...

WHAT'S THE MATTER?

IT'S THIS STUPID MATH PROBLEM. I DON'T KNOW WHERE TO BEGIN.

LEMME SEE.

I'VE BEEN WORKING ON IT ALL AFTERNOON.

WOW. I DON'T KNOW WHERE TO BEGIN...

HA! I'M NOT ALONE!

OK. SEE THIS "X"? IT'S CALLED A VARIABLE.

I THOUGHT THOSE WERE "TIMES" SIGNS...

SO WHAT'S THIS PROBLEM WORTH?

FIVE EXTRA CREDIT POINTS.

SO WHAT'S THAT WORTH?

HALF A QUIZ.

WHICH IS WORTH WHAT?

SOMETHING LIKE ONE PERCENT OF MY FINAL GRADE.

PAIGE, C'MON — IN DOLLARS.

I DUNNO. WHAT'D YOU CHARGE PETER FOR THAT LAB REPORT?

STUPID JASON.

WHAT IS IT NOW?

I HAVE THIS KILLER EXTRA CREDIT MATH PROBLEM TO DO AND HE WON'T GIVE ME THE STUPID ANSWER!

AND HE SHOULDN'T.

WHAT?!

PAIGE, IF SOMEONE JUST GIVES YOU THE ANSWER, YOU'RE NOT LEARNING ANYTHING. JASON'S DOING THE RIGHT THING.

FINE. CAN I BORROW $8?

WHAT FOR?

REMEMBER, I SAID CRISP BILLS...

DADDY, I NEED SOME HELP.

WITH?

I HAVE THIS EXTRA CREDIT MATH PROBLEM I CAN'T DO AND—...

WELL, YOU'VE CERTAINLY COME TO THE RIGHT PERSON! "SLIDE RULE" FOX THEY USED TO CALL ME BACK IN COLLEGE. MAN, OH MAN WAS I SHARP. SO HOW CAN I HELP?

AMEND

JASON WANTS $8 TO DO IT FOR ME.

THAT'S OK— I'LL DO IT FOR FREE. WHAT'S THE PROBLEM?

I DON'T HAVE $8.

WAIT RIGHT HERE—"SLIDE RULE'S" GONNA GO GET A PENCIL.

PLEEEE-EEASE?

PAIGE, I'M NOT GIVING YOU $8 SO YOU CAN PAY JASON TO DO YOUR MATH HOMEWORK!

BUT I NEED THE EXTRA CREDIT!

THEN DO IT YOURSELF.

I CAN'T! IT'S TOO HARD!

THEN I GUESS YOU'LL JUST HAVE TO TRY HARDER.

PLEEEE-EEASE?

I MEANT AT THE MATH.

AMEND

YOUR DELAY HAS COST YOU. I'VE UPPED MY PRICE TO 10 BUCKS.

TOO BAD. I'VE DECIDED TO DO THE PROBLEM MYSELF.

WHAT?! YOU'LL NEVER BE ABLE TO DO IT! YOU SAID YOUR-SELF IT WAS TOO TOUGH!

IT MAY VERY WELL BE TOO TOUGH. BUT MOM HAD A GOOD POINT— IF I'M GOING TO GET EXTRA CREDIT, I WANT IT TO BE BECAUSE I EARNED IT, NOT BECAUSE I PAID FOR IT.

AMEND

TWO BUCKS.

MOM ALSO SAID I MIGHT LEARN A THING OR TWO IN THE PROCESS...

WHAT'S WITH THE BIG SMILE?

ANDY, YOU'RE LOOKING AT A NEW ROGER FOX.

OH?

A ROGER FOX WITH BALANCE... A LEVEL HEAD... A SURE GRIP... A ROGER FOX WHO PLAYS TO **WIN**!

UH-HUH.

I KNOW, I KNOW, I'VE TRIED THIS BEFORE, BUT THIS TIME IT'S GONNA WORK. IT JUST FEELS SO **RIGHT**.

AMEND

SO WHAT'D THIS NEW PUTTER **COST**?

NOW KEEP IN MIND IT'S A MAVERICK MARK VII...

HEE HEE HEE.

WHAT'S SO FUNNY?

I JUST SET UP A GOLF DATE WITH FRED. I DIDN'T TELL HIM I HAVE A NEW PUTTER.

AND YOU FIND THAT AMUSING?

HE'S WALKING INTO A ROUT, ANDY! YOU **BET** I FIND IT AMUSING.

OF COURSE, I SUBTLY QUAD-RUPLED OUR USUAL WAGER...

I GUESS I SEE HOW THIS **COULD** BE FUNNY.

AMEND

ROGER, I'M GOING TO BED.

WAIT—YOU'VE GOT TO SEE THIS NEW PUTTER IN ACTION.

IT'S INCREDIBLE, ANDY. YOU WOULDN'T BELIEVE THE DIFFERENCE IT MAKES. HEE HEE—I'M GONNA **KILL** FRED ON THE GREENS.

PUTT!

THUMP THUMP THUMP **OW!**

HECK, JUST PUT FRED IN THE BASEMENT.

YOU KNOW, I DON'T THINK THIS FLOOR IS LEVEL.

AMEND

103

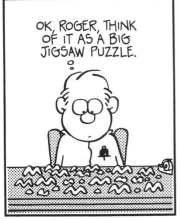

by Bill Amend

FoxTrot

A FIVE-LETTER WORD FOR "HUMILITY"...

A M N D

HMMM...

WHERE'S THE SUNDAY PAPER?

YOU'RE LOOKING AT IT.

WHAT DO YOU MEAN? WHERE'S THE SPORTS SECTION?

PETER'S GOT IT.

WHERE'S THE COMICS SECTION?

JASON'S GOT IT.

WHERE'S THE CROSSWORD PUZZLE?

I'VE GOT IT.

WHERE'S THE NEWS SECTION?

PAIGE'S GOT IT.

ALL THAT'S LEFT IS THIS STUPID HOME IMPROVEMENT SECTION!

ANDY, IS THIS ONE OF YOUR CUTE LITTLE HINTS?...

YOU GOT IT.

AMEND

FIVE DOWN IS "LYNX."

THIS ISN'T WHAT I MEANT...

WATER... I NEED WATER...

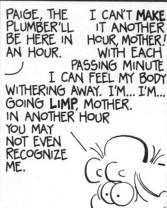

PAIGE, THE PLUMBER'LL BE HERE IN AN HOUR.

I CAN'T **MAKE** IT ANOTHER HOUR, MOTHER! WITH EACH PASSING MINUTE I CAN FEEL MY BODY WITHERING AWAY. I'M... I'M... GOING **LIMP**, MOTHER. IN ANOTHER HOUR YOU MAY NOT EVEN RECOGNIZE ME.

WATER... I NEED WATER...

HERE. HAVE A DIET COKE.

WHAT— I'M SUPPOSED TO SHAMPOO WITH **THIS**?

OK, YOU'RE BACK IN BUSINESS.

YOU FIXED THE VALVE?

YUP. PIECE O' CAKE.

THAT'S MY BILL.

EXPENSIVE CAKE.

OK, PIECE O' FERRARI.

EXPENSIVE FERRARI.

Lemonade $10 $209.49

Lemonade $10 $209.49

Lemonade $10 $209.49

I TAKE IT JASON COST US SOME MONEY TODAY.

BOARDING SCHOOL'S STARTING TO LOOK LIKE A BARGAIN.

AMEND

117

BOINK! **OW!**

SILLY PUTTY—
THE VERTICAL
BOOMERANG.

'COURSE NOW
IT'S ALL
GREASY.

MOTHER, WHERE'S
THAT LAWN-
DART SET?

JASON, I'M
HAVING TROUBLE
WITH THE VCR.

WHAT?
SETTING
THE
TIMER?

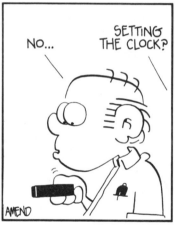

NO...

SETTING
THE CLOCK?

NO...

PLAYING
A TAPE?

TURNING IT ON.

WELL, FOR
STARTERS,
THAT'S THE
GARAGE
DOOR
OPENER.

**MY
CAR!**

THANKS.

WHAT'S WITH
THE EYEBROWS?

PAIGE
JUST
BORROWED
THE
NEWSPAPER.

SO?

SO OUR LITTLE GIRL
IS FINALLY SHOWING
AN INTEREST IN NEWS!
OUR LITTLE GIRL IS
FINALLY STARTING TO CARE
ABOUT CURRENT EVENTS! OUR
LITTLE GIRL IS FINALLY INTER-
ESTED IN LEARNING ABOUT
THE WORLD
SHE LIVES
IN!

OUR LITTLE GIRL
IS SPRAY-
PAINTING HER
OLD SNEAKERS.

GREAT.
AND SHE
TOOK THE
FUNNY
PAGES.

MOM, DID YOU EVER READ "THE RED BADGE OF COURAGE"?

SURE. WHY?

WELL, I'M SUPPOSED TO WRITE A PAPER ABOUT IT, AND—...

...AND YOU WANT ME TO REVIEW YOUR OUTLINE?

NO...

YOU WANT ME TO REVIEW YOUR ROUGH DRAFT?

I WANT YOU TO TELL ME WHAT THE BOOK'S ABOUT. IN DETAIL.

LET ME TELL YOU SOMETHING ELSE. IN DETAIL.

YOU WANT ME TO WHAT?!

HAVE ANOTHER KID. PLEEEEASE?

JASON, WHY?

SO I'D HAVE SOMEONE TO BEAT UP. SO I'D HAVE SOMEONE TO BOSS AROUND.

SO I'D HAVE SOMEONE TO PIN TO THE GROUND WHILST I DANGLE LOOGIES INCHES ABOVE THEIR NOSE.

COMPELLING AS YOUR REASONS MAY BE...

AND IF YOU DON'T WANT TO HAVE A GIRL, THAT'S FINE TOO.

NICOLE! JOSH MERCER ASKED ME OUT! CAN YOU BELIEVE IT?!

JOSH MERCER? THE JOSH MERCER?

HE'S CUTE... HE'S SMART... HE'S FUNNY... THIS SORT OF THING HAS NEVER HAPPENED TO ME BEFORE!

IT'S LIKE... IT'S LIKE... IT'S LIKE...

...A DREAM?

ZZZZ... EXACTLY...

HEY, PAIGE— WANNA SEE SOMETHING REALLY DISGUSTING?

WHAT IS IT?

I MEAN, REALLY, REALLY, **REALLY** DISGUSTING.

WHAT **IS** IT?

BLECH. YOU TELL **ME**.

AMEND

HENCE THE TERM "GAG."

JASON, THAT'S DISGUSTING.

CHECK.

CHECK?! THAT'S NOT CHECK!

ISN'T IT?

NO! ANDY, GEEZ— HOW MANY TIMES DO I HAVE TO **TEACH** YOU THIS GAME?!

AMEND

I MEAN, THIS MUST BE THE FIFTIETH TIME I'VE HAD TO GO OVER THE RULES WITH YOU! EITHER YOU'RE NOT PAYING ATTENTION OR YOU JUST DON'T HAVE THE SMARTS TO BE **PLAYING** CHESS. I MEAN, HOW CAN YOU CALL THIS "**CHECK**"?!

FINE. CHECK**MATE**.

FURTHERMORE, YOUR KNIGHT'S FACING THE WRONG WAY...

THE BASES ARE LOADED... PETER FOX WAITS FOR THE 3-AND-2 PITCH...

HE HITS A DEEP LINE DRIVE TO CENTER... WAY BACK... WAY BACK... IT'S **GONE!** A TWO-OUT GRAND SLAM!

PETER FOX HAS WON THE GAME!

AMEND

...AND LOST HIS MIND.

MVP? ME? WHY, THANK YOU...